All About Rabbits

Rachel McKay

Let's learn all about rabbits!

What do rabbits eat?

It's really important to make sure your pet rabbits have a healthy diet. This will help them to be happy and healthy bunnies!

Hay!

What is hay?

Hay is made by drying grass

Did you know?

A rabbit needs to eat their
own body size
in hay every single day!

Why rabbits need to eat hay:

- It keeps their tummy healthy
- It stops their teeth growing too long
- It's really fun to eat!

Most of what a rabbit eats should be hay.

Vegetables !

 Rabbits can eat a small amount of vegetables every day. Only some vegetables are safe for rabbits to eat!

Kale and spring green are safe for rabbits

Before you give your rabbits any type of fruit or veg, you need to check first if it's a safe food for them to eat

Did you know?

Rabbits like carrots, but they are not healthy for them. They should only get small pieces of carrot very occasionally as a treat

Fruit

Rabbits can eat very small amounts of some types of fruit. Apples and bananas are safe fruits for rabbits

They should only eat fruit sometimes as a treat - no more than once a week

Too much fruit or veg can make a rabbit very ill.

Pellets

Rabbits can eat a small amount of pellets every day.

What are pellets?

A crunchy food that rabbits love to eat. You can buy pellets from most pet stores.

Pellets can also be called **nuggets**

? Did you know?

Pellets give rabbits some extra nutrients that they can't get from hay and vegetables.

If you give your rabbits too many pellets, they won't eat enough hay.

This means that too many pellets can make your rabbits very unwell.

4

How fast can rabbits move?

In the wild, rabbits need to be able to hop really fast.
If they have enough space, pet rabbits can hop super fast too!

Super strong legs!

? ## Did you know?

An animal's back legs are also called their

hind legs

Rabbits have super strong back legs!

This helps them to push off the ground and hop really, really fast!

These strong legs also help them to jump and leap high in the air!

Rabbits can run as fast as **25mph**

Indoors

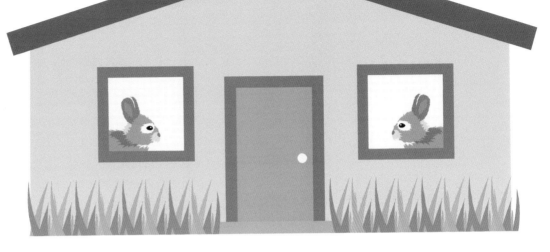

or outdoors?

Pet rabbits can live either inside or outside!

Indoor Rabbits

Rabbits

need to have

lots and lots of

space to hop

around and play!

They will love a big pen
or even a room to themselves

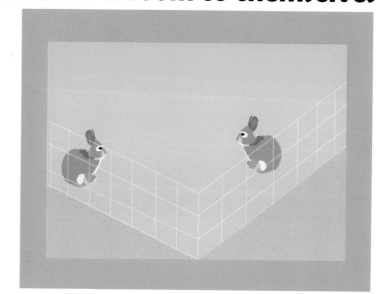

3m

2m

Rabbits need a space of
at least 2m x 3m so they
can get enough exercise

8

Outdoor Rabbits

● **A big run like this will help your bunnies get the exercise they need**

Just like indoor rabbits, outdoor rabbits also need a big space!

Outdoor bunnies also need somewhere to shelter from the weather

■ **The run also needs to be**

safe

✖ **So that your rabbits can't get out**

and

✖ **So that other animals can't get in**

Shelter

Outdoor rabbits need to be able to shelter from the wind and rain.

They also need to keep cool in warm weather and warm in cold weather.

A shed is a great way to give rabbits the shelter they need outside

tunnel

shed

run

Rabbits love to run along tunnels between their shed and their run

Prey or Predator?

Rabbits are prey animals.

This means that lots of other animals want to eat them!!!

Predators?

Predators are animals that eat other animals.

Prey?

Prey are animals that other animals want to eat.

This is why rabbits can be very nervous. When anything scares a rabbit, they feel as if they are about to be eaten!

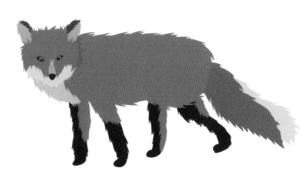

Animals like foxes are predators to rabbits.

If you have pet rabbits, you need to keep them safe from predators!

Why do rabbits thump?

When a rabbit thumps, they're not just making a noise, they're trying to tell you something is wrong!

Thumping

When rabbits thump they stamp their back legs as hard as they can on the ground.

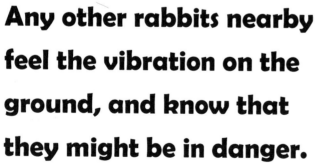

Any other rabbits nearby feel the vibration on the ground, and know that they might be in danger.

In the wild, rabbits thump to warn other rabbits of danger

If you hear your rabbits thumping, you should always check that they are ok – they're saying that something is wrong!

Baby Rabbits

Baby rabbits are born without fur, and they can't hear or see. So how do they get from being like this, to being a full grown bunny rabbit?

Newborn

2-7 days old

The rabbit's ears open and they can hear

7-12 days old

The rabbit will be covered in a thin layer of fur, and it's ears will start to stick up.

about 10 days

The rabbit's eyes will open and they will be able to see

about 3 weeks

They will start to eat some of their own food.

about 6 weeks

They will stop drinking their mother's milk, and will now be able to eat all of their own food

16

More about baby rabbits

Baby rabbits are born in groups called litters. Different breeds of rabbits can be more likely to have different sizes of litters.

Did you know?
Mother rabbits only feed their babies once or twice a day

A litter of baby rabbits can have anywhere from **1-8** babies in it.

Once female rabbits are about 3-4 months old, they are ready to have their own babies already!

Female rabbits can have a new litter of baby rabbits every few weeks!

A rabbit is fully an adult at about 6 months old.

Rabbits Growing Up

Giving a rabbit lots of space to play in as they grow up will help them to get stronger.

Giving a rabbit lots of toys to play with will help them to learn things and stop them from getting bored.

Giving a rabbit lots hay to eat, along with a very small amount of pellets and vegetables, will help them be healthy.

When do rabbits sleep?

Rabbits sleep in short naps, mostly during the day, but also during the night.

Rabbits sleep for around **8 hours** a day

Crepuscular?

Crepuscular animals are most active at dawn and dusk

Rabbits are most active at these times because this is when less of their predators are around.

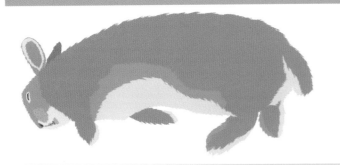

?

Did you know?

Rabbits can sleep with their eyes open, or with their eyes closed. This lets them keep a look out for any danger.

Rabbits Having Fun!

Some people think rabbits are boring animals, but they're so wrong!

Rabbits love to have fun!

Rabbits love squeezing themselves through tunnels.

They like to have things to jump on and off of.

They enjoy playing with toys that they can gnaw at, pick up and dig at.

They also love having things to sit in and dig around in.

Breeds of Rabbits

There are loads and loads of different breeds of rabbits!

Different breeds of rabbit:

- are more likely to have specific shades of fur

- have different lengths of fur

- have different body shapes

- are more likely to be a set size

For example

Rabbits who have long hair around their faces, and have thick fur, are called Lionhead rabbits. Lionhead rabbits are more likely to be quite small rabbits, and they can be a range of different shades

1 Bunny or 2 ?

Some pet rabbits live alone. Other pet rabbits, have a rabbit friend who lives with them. So, should rabbits live alone, or together?

Rabbits are very sociable animals, and they should always live with other rabbits.

Before rabbits can live together they need to 'bond' with each other.

Rabbits who have a rabbit friend will love playing together, and eating together

Bonded?

Rabbits who live together and are friends are called bonded rabbits.

Looking for more books like this one?

www.smallfurryfriends.com